WITCHES, WOLVES, AND WATER SPIRITS

Slavic Poems of Novgorod

Written and Illustrated

RAND DARROW

ALIONUSHKA'S SONG

["The Wedding of Love"]

I sing you this song
    Of love that is strong
And can't be denied
    No matter what goes wrong
A grape on the vine
    When turned into wine
Maturing with age
    Is better served with time
[chorus]
From mountains above
    To the sea down below
A true lasting love
    Will germinate and grow
Two lovers will stand
    A ring on their hand
Like the sun and the moon
    Forever they will glow
[chorus]
No matter how near
    No matter how far
Our love will be true
    No matter where we are
Two hearts that are one
    Can not be undone
Two rivers will flow
    Together they will run [chorus added]

CHORUS
  We'll laugh and sing
    And bells will ring
The sun will shine
    As people dine
The bride and groom
    Waltz round the room
In three quarter time

The birds soar high
    Up in the sky
A fish will jump
    To catch a fly
The deer will leap
    Through fields of rye
To celebrate our love

The wedding of love
The wedding of love
The wedding of love

DVINA'S SECRET

Dvina has a secret
      That she will not tell
And locks it in her heart
      Inside a wishing well
Somewhere within her smile
      Or deep in her blue eyes
I see her dark deception
      And her hidden lies

We spend our time together
      Telling one another
That we will be true
      But she is holding back
It seems as though there's something
      Lurking beneath the surface
That I can not see
      Dvina please tell me

Dvina has a secret
      That she will not tell
And locks it in her heart
      Inside a wishing well
Somewhere within her smile
      Or deep in her blue eyes
I see her dark deception
      And her hidden lies

We can't go on too long
       Pretending
This mystery must have
       An ending
Dvina, tell me what
       You're hiding
But when
       She stares at me
I feel my heart
       Is downward sliding

Dvina has a secret
       That she will not tell
And locks it in her heart
       Inside a wishing well

Now she has gone to sleep
       She closes her blue eyes
And I am left alone
       To see the pale moon rise

CHORUS
  (Dvina talk to me)
  (Dvina talk to me)
  (Dvina tell me what you know)

DO IT ALL AGAIN

[Sofia and Tanya Dance]

It's one two three
        Then turn around
And don't forget to bend
        Those supple arms
And keep them high
        Now do it all again

It's one two three
        Then turn around
And don't forget to bend
        My feet are sore
This is a chore
        When will this ever end

We've been at this
        Since early morn
We really need a break
        I feel my muscles
All have torn
        And, oh, does my back ache

You must continue
        Practicing
There is so much
        To learn

It takes hard work
       To reach a goal
That's how good things
       Are earned

It's one two three
       Then turn around
And don't forget to bend
       Those supple arms
And keep them high
       Now do it all again

It's one two three
       Now point those feet
And keep that leg up high
       The only winners
To compete
       Are those that always try

Oh what's the use
       Of practicing
We haven't got
       A chance
The others are
       More experienced
We'll never
       Win this dance

If you don't try
       To win this thing
And give it
       All you can

WITCHES, WOLVES, AND WATER SPIRITS

You'll never know
            What fate will bring
Now do it all again

It's one two three
            Then turn around
And don't forget to bend
            Those supple arms
And keep them high
            Now do it all again

It's one two three
            Now point those feet
And keep that leg up high
            The only winners
To compete
            Are those that always try

ELENA'S SONG

Since lost within a storm
       My husband just ignores me
He wakes up in the morn
       But he no longer greets me
Before he goes to bed
       He never wants to hug me
I might as well be dead
       The way he just neglects me

I married my true love
       In August
We had our life all planned
       Before us
Our love I thought would last
       Forever
But now he's not the same
       He doesn't know my name

He wakes up in the morn
       And he no longer greets me
How long will this go on?
       But he will never answer
I can not take this strain
       He never wants to kiss me
I think I'll go insane
       My husband doesn't love me

VASILISA CALLS ME

I'm lost within a storm
      My Vasilisa finds me
I wake up in the morn
      My Vasilisa greets me
Before I go to bed
      My Vasilisa hugs me
I think she's in my head
      Sweet Vasilisa calls me

I married my true love
      In August
We had our life all planned
      Before us
Our love I thought would last
      Forever
But then there came the dreams
      And nothing's what it seems

I wake up in the morn
      My Vasilisa greets me
How long will this go on?
      But she will never answer
I can not take this strain
      My Vasilisa sooths me
I think I'll go insane
      My Vasilisa's smiling

ETERNAL JOURNEY

Sometimes we make mistakes
    We can't always be right
It haunts us while awake
    And torments us at night
It's not your fault
    You're not to blame
Don't bow your head
    Because of shame
What happened
    Is the past
Don't try
    To make it last
The future never
    Stays the same

Tomorrow is
    Another day
Dark clouds will start
    To fade away
The golden sun
    Will shine
So leave
    The past behind
It's time that you
    Were on your way

The journey's there for you
    There's so much you can do

Don't hide your head
>   Beneath the covers
Spend your time
>   By helping others

And as you start
>   To build again
The wounds inside
>   Begin to mend
Your dreams
>   Will come alive
As you regain
>   Your pride
A journey that
>   Will never end

FEAR BABA YAGA

Oh fear Baba Yaga
       She's coming for you
And if she gets hold of you
       You will be through
She'll mash up your bones
       To put into her stew
There's no place to hide
       And there's nothing to do

She flies through the air
       On a mortar of doom
A pestle in one hand
       The other a broom
From out of the forest
       And out of the gloom
Baba Yaga
       Will find you
And then
       She will grind you

Oh fear Baba Yaga
       She's coming for you
And if she gets hold of you
       You will be through
She'll mash up your bones
       To put into her stew

There's no place to hide
    And there's nothing to do

With scraggly hair
    And a long crooked nose
She lives in the forest
    Where nobody goes
Her house is supported
    By two chicken legs
And circled by ivory
    Skulls that light up the night
Just like the Northern Lights

Oh fear Baba Yaga
    She's coming for you
And if she gets hold of you
    You will be through
She'll mash up your bones
    To put into her stew
There's no place to hide
    And there's nothing to do

If you go to visit her
    Be pure of soul
For if you are not
    You'll end up in her bowl
There are many rules
    That you should first learn
And if you don't follow them
    You won't return

Oh fear Baba Yaga
    She's coming for you

And if she gets hold of you
       You will be through
She'll mash up your bones
       To put into her stew
There's no place to hide
       And there's nothing to do

IN THE WAY

In the way
        In the way
Why is something always
        In the way?
Take today
        When I came to see him
I can't stay there long
        For someone comes who's
In the way

In the way
        In the way
Why is something always
        In the way?
Come what may
        I can't take control
Of things I do not know
        That happen to get
In the way

There are times
        When I would see his face
Across a room
        Inside a crowded place
And I think that he
        Would turn and notice me
But that is never quite the case

I have dreamt of him
> For all these years
But reality
> Just ends in tears
I can not convey
> The words I want to say
I'm shy and that
> Is in the way

In the way
> In the way
Why is something always
> In the way?
Skies are gray
> On the days
Which start at dawn
> And I know
He is gone
> He's left
And went away

In the way
> In the way
Why is something always
> In the way?
Yesterday
> I felt my heart yearn
When he did not return
> And I thought something's
In the way

Sometimes when I am sitting
> All alone

I dream he's sitting
           Next to me
We are the king and queen
           Upon our throne
And we are happy
           As can be

Our kingdom stretches out
           Before our eyes
To the mountains
           Far away
Then a loud noise
           Takes me by surprise
There's always something
           In the way

In the way
           In the way
Why is something always
           In the way?
Must obey
           Laws that say
That you are out
           If you should
Stray or doubt
           For that gets
In the way

In the way
           In the way
Why is something always
           In the way?
Life's a sleigh

Going down a hill
It's such a thrill until
It hits a rock that's
In the way

Now is my love
A fantasy?
And am I foolish
To go on?
Perhaps we're just
Not meant to be
Our hearts will never get
A chance to bond

Should I abandon
This crusade?
And let my true love
Fade away
Mistakes so often
Have been made
Oh! Why is something always
In the way?

In the way
In the way
Why is something always
In the way?
In the fray
Of a battle
In my heart
That my love's
Come apart
For something's
In the way

WITCHES, WOLVES, AND WATER SPIRITS

In the way
       In the way
Why is something always
       In the way?
Go away
       Don't ever come again
For this is now the end
       Of things that have been
In the way

ISLE OF BUYAN

Oh listen to me
         When I tell
The story of Buyan
           Across the ocean's mighty swell
And past the land beyond

An island secret
         To all men
Immortal's private lair
         A place where sky
And land will blend
         The gods will gather there

A sudden breeze
         Will shake the trees
The leaves cling to
         Their bending branches
And billowed clouds
         Race 'cross the sky
As wind begins
         To whip and blow
A storm approaches
         From the west
And stirs the sea
         Into a frenzy
The waves are crashing
         On the rocks
That line the shore below

The Isle of Buyan
              Wonder island
Far across the sea

The Isle of Buyan
              Wonder island
Place I wish to be

The Isle of Buyan
              Wonder island
Grows the Green Oak Tree

The Isle of Buyan
              Wonder island
Magic island
                    Scared island
Secret isle of mystery

Upon the hills
              Of forest green
A distant temple
              Can be seen
An amber stone
                    That lies alone
While water flows
              From down below
Clear rivers of
              The world begin
At Alatyr
              The stone within
And all the winds
              With all their force
They find their source
              From here

The Isle of Buyan
                Wonder island
Far across the sea

The Isle of Buyan
                Wonder island
Place I wish to be

The Isle of Buyan
                Wonder island
Grows the Green Oak Tree

The Isle of Buyan
                Wonder island
Magic island
                Sacred island
Secret isle of mystery

And now we're on
                A journey to
The Isle of Buyan
                Me and you
We will arrive
                As Kit shall drive
Us through the sea
                Of green and blue
And when we step
                Upon the shore
We'll see a land
                That you'll adore
And never will
                You want to leave
The Isle of Buyan

IVAN AND SAVA DANCE

I dance upon the land
    I dance upon the waves
From here you look so grand
    You're prince among the knaves
I see you down below
    I see you up above
You make my warm heart glow
    My everlasting love

Come dance with me
    Come dance with me
I feel the water's flow
    Romance with me
      Romance with me
    From shore to shore I go
Come dance with me
    Come dance with me
I cross a bridge of stone
    Romance with me
      Romance with me
    We both are on our own

Yet we are both a team
    I dance upon the stream
I dance upon the land
    But now we both hold hands

And so we dance apart
       Connecting at the heart
Converging at the shore
       Together evermore

It's time to part again
       The river's at my feet
I cut across its plane
       Like scissors through a sheet
The bridge connects two roads
       A heart beneath the breast
And carries heavy loads
       Connecting east and west

Come dance with me
       Come dance with me
I feel the water's flow
       Romance with me
          Romance with me
       From shore to shore I go

Come dance with me
       Come dance with me
I cross the bridge of stone
       Romance with me
          Romance with me
       We both are on our own

We dance just you and I
       Beneath the clear blue sky
But I fear something's wrong
       This moment won't last long

I see within your face
    A doubt I can't erase
What secret do you know
    What card do you not show

It's time to go again
    The river is my friend
We haven't time to waste
    I dance upon it's face
I dance upon the shore
    And to the bridge above
The girl that I adore
    Is Sava, my true love

Come dance with me
    Come dance with me
I feel the water's flow
    Romance with me
        Romance with me
    From shore to shore I go
Come dance with me
    Come dance with me
I cross the bridge of stone
    Romance with me
        Romance with me
    We both are on our own
Come dance with me
    Come dance with me
I feel the water's flow
    Romance with me
        Romance with me
    From shore to shore I go

Come dance with me
Come dance with me
I cross the bridge of stone
Romance with me
Romance with me
[Sava disappears beneath the water]
And now I'm all alone

KOLJADA SEASON

The winter solstice
        Has arrived
The longest night
        Is here
We're thankful that
        We're still alive
As we conclude
        The year
We bid the sun
        A quick good bye
You haven't long
        To stay
A brief appearance
        In the sky
The night will rule
        The day

The season of Koljada
        Conclusion of the year
A time of celebration
        Festivals and toasts of cheer

The season of Koljada
        Another year will end
It's time to bring the sun back
        A ring of fire we will tend

The season of Koljada
          A mask upon your face
Wandering from house to house
          Sing a song at every place

The season of Koljada
          Kozuli shaped like goats
And people celebrating
          With heavy boots and winter coats

The hearth is very sacred
          A ladder to the sky
The women sing and dance there
          To bring the sun up high
The days will now last longer
          The cold will melt away
The sun will be triumphant
          Blue skies replace the gray

The season of Koljada
          Conclusion of the year
A time of celebration
          Festivals and toasts of cheer

The season of Koljada
          Another year has past
It's time to bring the sun back
          And hope the winter will not last

KOSCHEI THE DEATHLESS

Koschei, Koschei
   He's a fox
Hides his soul
   Inside a box
Those who've crossed him
   They have died
Keeps his sabre
   By his side

Down from a castle
   On a mountain
Koschei rides
   His horse of white
His teeth clinched tight
   Red eyes so bright
On such
   A ghastly day
He waves his sword
   Above his head
As creatures
   Run away in dread
They all have fled
   He'd wake the dead
Now Koschei's
   On his way

Across the plains
   Of wheat and grains

Baking sun
            Torrential rains
And forest lush
            With thorns and brush
And pines all
            Green and blue
Oh Koschei drives
            His heaving horse
Upon this course
            With out remorse
And whips the beast
            He will not cease
Until this long hard
            Journey's through

Koschei, Koschei
            He's a fox
Hides his soul
            Inside a box
Those who've crossed him
            They have died
Keeps his sabre
            By his side

Down from a castle
            On a mountain
Koschei rides
            His horse of white
His teeth clinched tight
            Red eyes so bright
On such
            A ghastly day

He waves his sword
       Above his head
As creatures
       Run away in dread
They all have fled
       He'd wake the dead
Now Koschei
       On his way

Though Koschei
       Is immortal
And his soul
       Is locked away
He always fears
       That someone
Will discover it
       Someday
He tries to
       Keep it secret
And he doesn't
       Trust a soul
You never know
       Who's listening
And people
       Gossip so

Koschei, Koschei
       He's a fox
Hides his soul
       Inside a box
Those who've crossed him
       They have died

Keeps his sabre
> By his side

Down from a castle
> On a mountain
Koschei rides
> His horse of white
His teeth clinched tight
> Red eyes so bright
On such
> A ghastly day
He waves his sword
> Above his head
As creatures
> Run away in dread
They all have fled
> He'd wake the dead
Now Koschei's
> On his way

When he rides
> Into a village
All the people
> Start to flee
They lock their doors
> And windows
Then they
> Throw away the key
They hope that
> He will soon depart
And leave them
> All alone

While they huddle
        All together
Safe inside
        Their humble homes

Koschei, Koschei
        He's a fox
Hides his soul
        Inside a box
Those who've crossed him
        They have died
Keeps his sabre
        By his side

LOCK AWAY LOVE

I can not let you go
              And maybe you don't understand
I know I love you so
              You are my only man

My love I lock away
              To save another day
Together run away
              To start a life somewhere alone

When troubles all have gone
              And darkness fades to dawn
It's time that we move on
              To start a journey on our own

Some day
              When we're together
We'll take a trip
              Across the sea
We may
              Meet stormy weather
But we'll persist
              Just you and me

We'll see
              A new tomorrow

Adventures in
> Forbidden lands

Good bye
> To days of sorrow

We'll drink fine wine
> While holding hands

My love I lock away
> To save another day

Together run away
> To start a life somewhere alone

When troubles all have gone
> And darkness fades to dawn

It's time that we move on
> To start a journey on our own

Today is filled with wonder
> How will my life unfold?

And if my actions blunder
> Will all my plans erode?

I can't go on without him
> What would I ever do?

And though success is so slim
> My faith I must hold true

My love I lock away
> To save another day

Together run away
> To start a life somewhere alone

When troubles all have gone
        And darkness fades to dawn
It's time that we move on
        To start a journey on our own

I know that life is harsh
        And forces us to struggle
We wallow through the marsh
        And sometimes we get lost

The time we are apart
        Will help to make us stronger
But love that's in my heart
        Can't be denied
For too much longer

My love I lock away
        To save another day
Together run away
        To start a life somewhere alone

When troubles all have gone
        And darkness fades to dawn
It's time that we move on
        To start a journey on our own
           [Today is filled with wonder]

LOST IN THE UNDERWORLD

I'm lost inside the Underworld
     And can not find my way
I'm lost inside the Underworld
     And everything is charcoal gray
I'm lost inside the Underworld
     And haven't got a friend
I'm lost inside the Underworld
     And won't see home again

The world I knew
     Is filled with love
And life is all around
     I wish that I
Was up above
     And not beneath the ground
The sun's warm rays
     Upon my face
Would help revive my soul
     But I am lost
Inside this place
     And I don't know
Which way to go

I'm lost inside the Underworld
     And can not find my way
I'm lost inside the Underworld
     And everything is charcoal gray

I'm lost inside the Underworld
>When will this ever end?
I'm lost inside the Underworld
>And won't see home again

If I escape
>And leave this strife
I'll thank my lucky stars
>No one could have
A richer life
>Not even all the czars
And in the evening
>When the sun
Is setting then it's gone
>I'll wait until
The night is done
>Then welcome it at dawn

I'm lost inside the Underworld
>And can not find my way
I'm lost inside the Underworld
>And everything is charcoal gray
I'm lost inside the Underworld
>Where will this journey end?
I'm lost inside the Underworld
>And won't see home again

MAGIC CARPET FIELD OF GOLD

The sun shines on my face
              So warm and bright
The breeze flows through my hair
              So soft and light
The scent of morning flowers
              Fills my head
As spring awakens
              From its bed
The winter snows
              Have melted in the ground
The clouds are gone
              The fields alive
And buzzing's all around

Just let your dreams decide
              Your destiny
And swing yourself around
              So gracefully
A castle's in the distance
              Not too far
While you are waltzing
              With a Czar
It's time to find
              A partner you can hold
And dance around and dance around
              In a carpet field of gold

And so you catch a carriage
> To the sun

For you and royal husband
> Now are one

A life of endless blessings
> You'll enjoy

A girl for you
> For him a boy

And as you age
> The years will fade away

Then you will find
> Your love will bind

Forever and a day

So let your dreams decide
> Your destiny

And dance with your true love
> So gracefully

For you and he will waltz
> Until you're old

In a magic carpet field of gold

MASLENITSA

What a wonderful day
      In the forest deep
You can hear the newborn
      Sparrows peep
And the moss on the trees
      Is an emerald green
That is velvet soft
      Just for a queen

A trickling brook
      Meanders over stones
While chipmunks chatter
      As they gather sticky cones

In a field stands a doe
      With her baby fawn
They've been grazing
      Since the break of dawn
And Lada has arrived
      From the frozen earth
As she brings forth
      Spring and new rebirth

Oh, it's time to celebrate
      The birth of spring
Maslenitsa don't be late
      We all will sing

And to cleanse away the old
            Will bring the new
Decorated eggs are rolled
            Now winter's through

It's a wonderful day
            In the forest deep
I feel so alive
            I can not sleep
Such a heavenly scene
            In the early spring
Now we've freed ourselves
            From winter's cling

MY FRUSTRATION

Sometimes I find
              Myself alone
And thinking how
              The world's unfair
My heart is sinking
              Like a stone
Into a stream
              Of deep despair
Then dragged into
              The currents flow
Where will it take me?
              I don't know
A spinning leaf
              Without control
My mind is slowly
              Letting go

I know I shouldn't
              Feel this way
And count my blessings
              Every day
But then frustration
              Builds again
I think of things
              I can not do
And feel as though
              I have no friend

Who comprehends?
                    Of what I go through

To live a life
                    Of no restraint
And dance until
                    Your hearts content
I know it's selfish
                    To complain
Forgive me please
                    I need to vent

I dream someday
                    That I might dance
And maybe dabble
                    With romance
Together we would
                    Both hold hands
And travel to
                    Exotic lands

But I must face
                    Reality
How can these dreams
                    Come true for me?
Oh, I am but
                    A crippled soul
Without a future
                    Or a goal
For me it's just
                    A futile chance
That I would ever
                    Find romance

That's not for me
                    But just for you
Who are among
                    The privileged few

To take what life may give
                    Is what they say
But I find that I live
                    From day to day
Don't let life pass you bye
                    Participate
Why should I even try?
                    It's way too late

There are those days
                    It's hard to live
I struggle just
                    To stay alive
I've given all
                    I have to give
And emptied all
                    The tears I've cried

I see my problem's
                    Here to stay
It doesn't seem
                    To go away
There isn't much
                    For me to say
I guess tomorrow
                    Is another day
I think I'll try to
                    Sleep on it awhile

NOVGOROD

The air is brisk
        The frost it bites
On wintry nights
        In Novgorod
The wind will howl
        The clouds will scowl
Hold tight your cowl
        In Novgorod
Stribog whips
        A gust that chills
Across the hills
        Of Novgorod
The days are short
        The nights are long
We sing this song
        Of Novgorod

The houses are ruff wood
        In Novgorod
In mighty storms they stood
        In Novgorod
The people all do good
        In Novgorod
And pray as they all should
        In Novgorod

When April sun rays
          Melt the snow
And rushing rivers
          Start to flow
The frozen land
          Will warm and thaw
Dry seeds will fall
          Then start to grow
The gray spring clouds
          Begin to rain
Across the flat
          And empty plain
The farmers pray
          Their fields will drain
They'll all complain
          In Novgorod

In Novgorod
          Spring still moves on
Yarilo waves
          His magic wand
And everything
          Turns apple green
It's such a warm
          And pleasant scene

The tales are old
          Of Novgorod
They tell of Slavensk's
          Tragic souls
Who fought and battled
          Nature's foes
They played their role
          In Novgorod

Volkhov River
        Roll along
As Sadko plays
        His lonesome song
And toss a coin
        For Ole Perun
His days are done
        In Novgorod

[In Novgorod, In Novgorod, In Novgorod]

At summer time
        In Novgorod
Another world
        Appears
I watch it form
        A fantasy
And wash away
        My fears
The things I want
        To happen
Will occur
        Before my eyes
I see a field
        That's filled with joy
And love birds
        Fill the skies

At summer time
        In Novgorod
Lake LImen's
        Blue and clear

The forest starts

        To come alive

With antelope

        And deer

The squirrels are chattering

        In the trees

The mice are

        Nibbling grain

The old gray wolf

        Is itching flees

A spider

        Catches rain

And now the leaves

        Are turning red

And yellow, orange

        And brown

It won't be long

        Till winter comes

As snow flakes fall

        Without a sound

A year's gone by

        In Novgorod

The weather's

        Damp and cold

We sit around

        The hearth at night

To hear a tale

        Of old

A story about

        Ole Novgorod

And heroes

        Of the past

And how they fought
>> For what was right

Forever
>> They will last

The air is brisk
>> The frost it bites

On wintry nights
>> In Novgorod

The wind will howl
>> The clouds will scowl

Hold tight your cowl
>> In Novgorod

Stribog whips
>> A gust that chills

Across the hills
>> Of Novgorod

The days are short
>> The nights are long

We sing this song
>> Of Novgorod

RUSAL'NAYA FESTIVAL

It's time to leave your watery home
        In fields and forest you will roam
To dance a khorovod at night
        A summer's moon delight
With poppy garlands in your hair
        The trees are now your new found lair
You try to coax your victims there
        And steal away their souls

Into the forest green
        Young women will be seen
Bright flowers they will tie
        On birch trees they can spy
Oh curl a young birch tree
        And tie it to the ground
Then stripping off its leaves
        You make a birch wreath crown

Semickajas
        Semickajas
Semickajas
        Are sung
The sacred birch
        Is ritually
Into the river
        Flung
Semickajas

Semickajas

Semickajas

Are sung

The sacred birch

Is ritually

Into the river

Flung

It's time we must deliver

Wreaths into the river

As they float away

We wave goodbye

And those that float downstream

Will grant their lovers dream

And in a full years time

The wedding bells will chime

And now it's time to call an end

To Rusal'naya week my friend

The rituals have been performed

Now crops will start to grow

We sang and danced

And had our feast

Rusalki spirits

Are at peace

The leaves are rustling

In the wind

Let summertime begin

SLAVENSK

It's time to say
>   Good bye to Slavensk
Oh what on earth
>   Are we to do?
There's never going to be
>   Another
We'll have to start
>   Anew
The sun would shine
>   It's rays on Slavensk
The skies were always
>   Crystal blue
The fragrance of
>   The many flowers
Along the streets
>   They grew

The festivals
>   In Slavensk
Were colorful
>   And bright
The people
>   Liked to dress up
And dance
>   All through the night
Remember all
>   The laughter

And everything
                    Seemed right
Oh look what's
                    Happened after
When will we
                    See the light?

Now gather all
                    Your things together
The memories
                    You had before
It's time to face
                    The stormy weather
And head on
                    Out the door
The village we once
                    Shared as Slavensk
Is still ingrained
                    Within our mind
But now those days
                    Are over
A memory
                    In time

SONG OF THE RUSALKI

When the evening succumbs
                    To the shadows of night
And the candles are lit
                    With the doors fastened tight
There's a feeling inside of me
                    Waiting to go
It whispers commands
                    That tug strings at my soul

From far down below
                    Where silver fish compete
To scour for food
                    And find enough to eat
A fever that burns
                    So deep inside my head
Demands I return
                    To river of the dead

Where spirits roam
                    Beneath the foam
Of rapid waters spray
                    From rocks that block their way
They twist and dive
                    Past fish alive
That never see them pass
                    Because they move too fast

They sweep to the bottom
> Of the river bed
Where caverns and caves
> Form castles of the dead
Rusalki reside
> In a murky olive lair
Though no other creature
> Ever ventures there

And life above
> Is fast to sleep
The farmer snores in bed
> His wife is counting sheep
But rusalki's world
> Is green and dark
They prowl the river shores
> Just like the tiger shark

The song of rusalki
> Swimming down below
Is sung by the currents
> Of the river flow
Which carry swift waters
> From mountains and plain
That drift to the sea
> But shall return again
>> And again
>> And again
>> And again

THE DREAM

I'm lying here
        Alone in bed
Beside me
        Is a book I read
My eyes are tired
        And turning red
I close them
        And the world
Is fading

The sounds
        Outside my window pane
Are whirling 'round
        Inside my brain
And what once was
        Is not the same
I'm on my way
        And now my dream begins

I'm in a land
        Of make believe
With colors
        All around
The sky is down
        Below my feet
Above
        There is the ground

And caught

        Inside a rubber ball

That's bouncing

        Up and down

I crash

        Right through

A window pane

        And never

Make a sound

I'm lying here

        Alone in bed

Beside me

        Is a book I read

My eyes are tired

        And turning red

I close them

        And the world

Is fading

The sounds

        Outside my window pane

Are whirling 'round

        Inside my brain

And what once was

        Is not the same

I'm on my way

        And dreaming once again

I'm now inside

        A castle wall

There's glass

        Upon the floor

And drifting down
           A checkered hall
I stand before a door

Behind, a latch
           Is quickly pulled
And hinges start to creak
           The door is slowly opened
And a voice
           Begins to speak

I'm lying here
           Alone in bed
Beside me
           Is a book I read
My eyes are tired
           And turning red
I close them
           And the world
Is fading

The sounds
           Outside my window pane
Are whirling 'round
           Inside my brain
And what once was
           Is not the same
I'm on my way
           And dreaming once again

Please come inside
           And close the door

We have no time to waste
                    And as I shut the door I heard
A lock snap into place

Then laughter blares
                    From up above
A joke's been played on me
                    You've locked yourself
Inside this place
                    It's called
Eternity

I'm lying here
                    Alone in bed
Beside me
                    Is a book I read
My eyes are tired
                    And turning red
I close them
                    And the world
Is fading

The sounds
                    Outside my window pane
Are whirling 'round
                    In side my brain
And what once was
                    Is now the same
I'm trapped inside my dream
                    Forever more

TIME TO REJOICE

It's time to rejoice!
        It's time to relax
Forget all your troubles
        And bury the axe
Let's gather with friends
        And slaughter a beast
Then build up a fire
        And have a feast

We'll toast to the left
        We'll toast to the right
We'll toast through the evening
        And toast through the night
Oh lift up your cup
        And sing out a song
As we celebrate
        The whole night long

Dark clouds disappear
        The sky is swept clear
No anguish and fear
        As we live our lives
So wipe away tears
        From previous years
And let out those cheers
        A new day arrives

It's time to rejoice!
        The music will play
We'll sing and we'll dance
        To the end of the day
We'll have a parade
        And march through the street
Then people will clap
        And jump to their feet

The children will shout
        And run after friends
Now everyone's out
        And we're happy again
There's joy that we share
        The skies are now fair
The best days are here
        Good bye despair

Dark clouds disappear
        The sky is swept clear
No anguish and fear
        As we live our lives
So wipe away tears
        From previous years
And let out those cheers
        A new day arrives

It's time to rejoice
        Oh isn't life grand!
We'll celebrate our joy
        Throughout all the land
Let all the world know
        How happy we are

And they can join in
      From near and far

It's time to rejoice!
      Our future looks bright
We've struggled for ages
      From terror and fright
With honor and pride
      We now can all say
We've worked side by side
      To bring this day

      It's time to rejoice!
      It's time to rejoice!
      It's time to rejoice!
      It's time to rejoice!

UPON A BRIDGE

I stand upon a bridge
    And stare into the water
Gurgling down below
    Into the undertow
One side there is a road
    That leads into my past
The other to a future
    That I'll never know
There was a time before
    When life was filled with light
And she stood by the door
    To welcome me inside at night
But now there's emptiness
    Wherever I may turn
The flame that lit my heart
    No longer does it burn
I stand upon a bridge
    And stare into the water
Gurgling down below
    It comes to take my soul

VASILISA AND THE WOLVES

We stalk
    We creep
        While you
            Are asleep
In shadows
    Black
        We poise
            To attack
With teeth
    So white
        They blaze
            In the night
Hooowl!
            We chase the weasel

You run
    You jump
        You trip
            On a stump
You zig
    You zag
        To escape
            From the hag
We're on
    Your trail
        And we
            Will not fail

Hooowl!
> We chase the weasel

Please, go away!
> Please, go away!
>> I'll not return
>>> Again

Don't go, my dear
> You need not fear
>> We want to be
>>> Your friend

Please, go away!
> Please, go away!
>> I need to get
>>> Back home

We wouldn't want
> You to get lost
>> And wander
>>> All alone

We stalk
> We creep
>> While you
>>> Are asleep

In shadows
> Black
>> We poise
>>> To attack

With teeth
> So white
>> They blaze
>>> In the night

Hooowl!
> We chase the weasel

You run
    You jump
        You trip
            On a stump
You zig
    You zag
        To escape
            From the hag
We're on
    Your trail
        And we
            Will not fail
Hooowl!
        We chase the weasel

Oh, how can I
    Escape from all
        The trouble
            That I'm in?
Poor Vasilisa
    Please slow down
        You fell and
            Hurt your shin
Oh look! The river
    Just before
        Is frozen
            Hard as stone

If I could reach
    The other shore
        I think I'll
            Be back home

We stalk
　　We creep
　　　　While you
　　　　　　Are asleep
In shadows
　　Black
　　　　We poise
　　　　　　To attack
With teeth
　　So white
　　　　They blaze
　　　　　　In the night
Hooowl!
　　　　We chase the weasel
You run
　　You jump
　　　　You trip
　　　　　　On a stump
You zig
　　You zag
　　　　To escape
　　　　　　From the hag
We're on
　　Your trail
　　　　And we
　　　　　　Will not fail
Hooowl!
　　We've got you now!

VOLKODLAK WALTZ

I think about the way
        You dance tonight
Especially the way
        You hold me tight
There's something that I feel
        Is not quite right
That tingle in my spine
        It comes from fright

I see the chill
        That's on your face
And I am trapped
        In your embrace
As we both waltz
        Within our space
The music still plays on
        I waltz around
The room with you
        But there is little
I can do
        To stop the terror
In my heart
        That I must leave
And be apart

I think about the way
        You dance tonight

Especially the way
      You hold me tight
There's something that I feel
      Is not quite right
That tingle in my spine
      It comes from fright

My hands are cold
      And start to shake
My nerves are frayed
      And start to break
How much more of this
      Can I take
Before this dance is through?

Around, around the floor
      We dance
I feel as though
      I'm in a trance
I can't escape
      There is no chance
Oh, what am I to do?

I think about the way
      You dance tonight
Especially the way
      You hold me tight
There's something that I feel
      Is not quite right
That tingle in my spine
      It comes from fright

And as the music
       Starts to slow
The lights are dimmed
       And turned down low
Who is this person?
       I don't know
He holds my hand
       And won't let go

Oh could this be a dream
       That's in my head
With feelings caught inside
       Of fear and dread
There's something that
       I feel is not quit right
The Volkodlak Waltz is
       My dance tonight

VOLOS

There is a god
                In Slavic lore
Who rules
                The land below
And toward Perun
                He has a score
To settle
                With his foe

And all the battles
                Fought before
Just made
                Their hatred grow
What does their future
                Have in store
No one
                Could ever know

He's the ruler of
                The Underworld
And Volos is his name
                The protector of
The flock of goats
                And cattle on the plain

He's the patron of
                Fine poetry

And art and oaths and trade
        A wolf, a serpent,
And a goat
        He often has portrayed

You must always
        Give him offerings
To keep him
        On your side
And never try his patience
        If you want to stay alive

One trip into
        The Underworld
And you will not return
        He'll throw you
In the Pit of Death
        Forever you will burn

For as long as all the stars have shined
        He's run this sacred place
No leader could be so sublime
        And rule with so much grace

He's the champion of all the gods
        The winner of the race
His reputation can't be flawed
        And he has such perfect taste

He's the ruler of
        The Underworld
And Volos is his name
        The protector of

The flock of goats
And cattle on the plain

He's the patron of
Fine poetry
And art and oaths and trade
A wolf, a serpent,
And a goat
He often has portrayed

You must always
Give him offerings
To keep him
On your side
And never try his patience
If you want to stay alive

One trip into
The Underworld
And you will not return
He'll throw you
In the Pit of Death
Forever you will burn

He helps to keep the cattle safe
On cold December nights
The animals look up to him
To be their guiding light

And if you take an oath to him
You better keep your word
For if you break your word to him
Your death will be assured

He's the ruler of

        The Underworld

And Volos is his name

        The protector of

The flock of goats

        And cattle on the plain

He's the patron of

        Fine poetry

And art and oaths and trade

        A wolf, a serpent,

And a goat

        He often has portrayed

You must always

        Give him offerings

To keep him

        On your side

And never try his patience

        If you want to stay alive

One trip into

        The Underworld

And you will not return

        He'll throw you

In the Pit of Death

        Forever you will burn

WATER BUG DANCER
[SAVA'S SONG]

Supported by my crutch
       My legs they have no touch
I hardly walk at all
       Without them I would fall
But hidden in my mind
       There's something that I find
Which limits can't control
       That lives within the soul

A melody
       Inside of me
Is whispering
       That I am free
No doors are locked
       I have the key
To go beyond my dreams
       The ropes that held me
All my life
       Are cut to ribbons
By a knife
       Like water bugs
On river glass
       I dance away
I'm free at last

I can not be confined
        And leave the land behind
Beyond the river's shore
        A world is mine
I glide across a sheet
        Of water at my feet
It glimmers in the sun
        I've just begun

The river is my floor
        Its surface my feet score
And patterns that I leave
        A water web I weave
As ripples form a V
        I can't believe it's me
An endless skipping stone
        And dancing all alone

A melody
        Inside of me
Is whispering
        That I am free
No doors are locked
        I have the key
To go beyond my dreams
        The ropes that held me
All my life
        Are cut to ribbons
By a knife
        Like water bugs
On river glass
        I dance away
I'm free at last

I can not be confined
       And leave the land behind
Beyond the river's shore
       The world is finally mine
I glide across a sheet
       Of water at my feet
It glimmers in the sun
       And now my heart has won

WOLVES BEHIND TREES

A rustling bush
  A crackling twig
Oh what could
  That sound be
An Owl hoots
  A field mouse scoots
Beneath an
  Old oak tree
The wind is gusting
  Leaves are hustling
Across a field
  Of grain
The forest sounds
  Are all around
And driving
  Me insane

We're wolves behind the trees
  And nobody knows we're here
We're wolves behind the trees
  And we'll fill your mind with fear
We're wolves behind the trees
  And we know just where you are
If you try to escape
  We won't let you get too far

We're wolves behind the trees
       And nobody knows we're here
We're wolves behind the trees
       And we'll fill your mind with fear
We're wolves behind the trees
       And we're going to get your goat
When you are not aware
       We'll spring out and grab your throat

It's too late to turn back now
       I'm afraid you've gone too far
You're our sacrificial cow
       And you're trapped just like a fly on tar

We're wolves behind the trees
       And nobody knows we're here
We're wolves behind the trees
       And we'll fill your mind with fear
We're wolves behind the trees
       And we know just where you are
If you try to escape
       We won't let you get too far

POMPOUS AFFAIR

It's time to gather all together
        The high elite around the land
We can't allow for stormy weather
        This program must be grand

The very best is what we choose from
        The service must meet every need
Expenses will be quite a high sum
        If we are to succeed

Accommodations must be perfect
        No stone will be left overturned
The help will always be there to check
        On anyone's concern

If there is any sort of complaint
        The problem will be rectified
And everything must be just so quaint
        They'll all be satisfied

There are a lot of preparations
        Before our honored guests arrive
We'll thoroughly check reservations
        So no one is denied

Mistakes will not be tolerated
        Excuses unacceptable

Our problems will be all abated
        If they are comfortable

The candles must be lit
        The firewood get split
Furniture be dusted
        Armor all derusted
Tapestries adjusted
        Fix the chair that's busted
But that's not the end

The silver must be polished
        Dirt and grime abolished
Filthy floors made shining
        Where they will be dining
Plates of golden trimming
        Filled with food that's brimming
And meetings to attend

When everything has been completed
        And all the guests start to appear
Our manners will not be impeded
        To obey them must be clear

What ever they may wish we'll do it
        No argument shall be allowed
If there's a problem then remove it
        The crisis will be solved

They'll all be dressed in formal wear
        So sparkling like a star
No mortal's garment could compare
        To the grandeur that they are

Gold and diamonds glistening
        With rubies red as fire
The luxury of all the kings
        And every man's desire

And now they gather all together
        The high elite around the land
Dressed in silk and finest leather
        Oh don't they look so grand

Magnificent just like a painting
        Everyone putting on airs
I hope there won't be any fainting
        I love pompous affairs

THE MUSIC BOX WALTZ

An old music box
  Upon a shelf
It stood all alone
  All by itself
One hinge had rust
  And cloaked in dust
Oh none had tried
  To see what's inside

Oh hear me play
  My magical sweet song
Your life is freed
  And nothing will go wrong
Your dread and fear
  That bothers you today
Will disappear
  And never come your way

So many long years
  Had all passed by
And the old music box
  Was moved up high
Upon the shelf
  All by itself
And none had tried
  To see what's inside

Oh hear me play
      My magical sweet song
Your life is freed
      And nothing will go wrong
Your dread and fear
      That bothers you today
Will disappear
      And never come your way

Well the old music box
      Had now been sold
To a little thin man
      Who was very old
He placed it down
      And opened the top
The music poured out
      And it never would stop

Oh hear me play
      My magical sweet song
Your life is freed
      And nothing will go wrong
Your dread and fear
      That bothers you today
Will disappear
      And never come your way

The old man just left
      But closed the lid
He'd been totally deaf
      Since he was a kid
The box remained
      Upon the shelf

And no one came
      It stood by itself

Oh hear me play
      My magical sweet song
Your life is freed
      And nothing will go wrong
Your dread and fear
      That bothers you today
Will disappear
      and never come your way

ACROSS THE TABLE

I'm dining with my love tonight
        She sits across the table
We have our meal by candlelight
        The food is good the mood is right
From distant shadows music plays
        A tune we find familiar
We toast a glass of ruby wine
        I hold her hand and she is mine

We waltz across the floor
        As though on ice
Together we are one
        In paradise
The music draws me back
        Into the past
A time that I believed
        Would always last

But now it's time for her to leave
        She gets up from the table
I feel my sad heart start to grieve
        I wipe my tears upon my sleeve
She fades into the morning mist
        For now she must move on
She turns and blows a parting kiss
        A subtle wave, and then she's gone

OUR SONG

We play this song
        And we both sing along
Just you and me
        In soft harmony

We drift around
        As though on a cloud
And play our song
        But not very loud

We play this song
        For you and for me
Together lost
        In our melody

It takes us to
        A time of our own
We linger there
        Until we come home

It's fun to spend
        This moment of time
Just writing lyrics
        And making them rhyme

The music that
        We play for our ears

Will never fade
> Throughout all the years

So nice to sing
> Together again

Oh, it's just a shame
> This song has to end

OUR GLORY

It's time to take a stand
        Our glory starts today
Raise high your sword in hand
        For victory's on it's way
We'll fight to the last man
        For what we know is right
There's nothing that
        Can stop us now
Until we win this fight

Our mission we'll complete
        With gallantry and might
The foes that we defeat
        Will run away in flight
The courage that we show
        Won't ever be forgot
We strike a lasting blow
        Till enemies are not

It's time to take a stand
        Our glory starts today
Raise high your sword in hand
        For victory's on it's way
We'll fight to the last man
        For what we know is right
There's nothing that
        Can stop us now

Until we win this fight

The battle lines are forming
        The time for truth is here
Defenses we'll be storming
        And we will not show fear
The enemy is stronger
        But we must stand our ground
If we persist much longer
        We're sure to bring them down

It's time to take a stand
        Our glory starts today
Raise high your sword in hand
        For victory's on it's way
We'll fight to the last man
        For what we know is right
There's nothing that
        Can stop us now
Until we win this fight

The battle rages yonder
        The day turns into night
It beckons you to ponder
        Is there an end in sight?
But dust clouds soon are parted
        The turmoil starts to quell
The quest that we had started
        Finds victory in hell

It's time to take a stand
        Our glory starts today
Raise high your sword in hand
        For victory's on it's way